The Anasazi Culture at
Mesa Verde

Sabrina Crewe and Dale Anderson

Gareth Stevens Publishing

A WORLD ALMANAC EDUCATION GROUP COMPANY

Please visit our web site at: www.garethstevens.com
For a free color catalog describing Gareth Stevens Publishing's list of high-quality
books and multimedia programs, call 1-800-542-2595 (USA) or 1-800-387-3178
(Canada). Gareth Stevens Publishing's fax: (414) 332-3567.

Library of Congress Cataloging-in-Publication Data

Crewe, Sabrina.
    The Anasazi culture at Mesa Verde / by Sabrina Crewe and Dale Anderson.
        p. cm. — (Events that shaped America)
    Includes bibliographical references and index.
    Summary: Discusses the cliff dwellings of Mesa Verde, Colorado, and what is known
about the history and culture of the Anasazi Indians who lived in them.
    ISBN 0-8368-3390-2 (lib. bdg.)
    1. Pueblo Indians—Colorado—Mesa Verde National Park—Antiquities—Juvenile literature.
2. Pueblo Indians—Colorado—Mesa Verde National Park—History—Juvenile literature.
3. Cliff dwellings—Colorado—Mesa Verde National Park—Juvenile literature. 4. Mesa Verde
National Park (Colo.)—Antiquities—Juvenile literature. [1. Pueblo Indians. 2. Indians of
North America—Southwest, New. 3. Mesa Verde National Park (Colo.)] I. Anderson,
Dale, 1953- . II. Title. III. Series.
    E99.P9C844   2003
    978.8'27—dc21   2002030997

First published in 2003 by
Gareth Stevens Publishing
A World Almanac Education Group Company
330 West Olive Street, Suite 100
Milwaukee, WI 53212 USA

Copyright © 2003 by Gareth Stevens Publishing.

Produced by Discovery Books
Editor: Sabrina Crewe
Designer and page production: Sabine Beaupré
Photo researcher: Sabrina Crewe
Maps and diagrams: Stefan Chabluk
Gareth Stevens editorial direction: Mark J. Sachner
Gareth Stevens art direction: Tammy Gruenewald
Gareth Stevens production: Jessica Yanke

Photo credits: Corbis: cover, pp. 4, 6, 7, 8, 9, 10, 11, 12, 13, 14, 15, 16, 17, 18–19, 20, 21,
22, 23, 24, 25, 26, 27.

Printed in the United States of America

1 2 3 4 5 6 7 8 9 07 06 05 04 03

Contents

Introduction

Mesa Verde covers about 120 square miles (310 square kilometers). In places, the mesa rises over 2,000 feet (600 meters) above the land around it.

What Is Mesa Verde?

In a corner of Colorado, Mesa Verde rises up like a giant table made of rock, many miles wide. Its name comes from two Spanish words. A *mesa*—Spanish for "table"—is a plateau, which is a large, raised piece of land. *Verde* is Spanish for "green," and the mesa is covered by a carpet of green trees.

 ## The Four Corners

Mesa Verde is in a part of the United States called the Four Corners. The region surrounds the point where the borders of four states—Colorado, Utah, Arizona, and New Mexico—meet. It is the only place in the United States where four states join in this way.

A place covered by green trees is unusual in the Four Corners area where Mesa Verde lies. It is very beautiful there, with wonderful red rocks cut into amazing shapes by wind and water. The region is very dry, however, and that makes it a difficult place to live and for plants and trees grow.

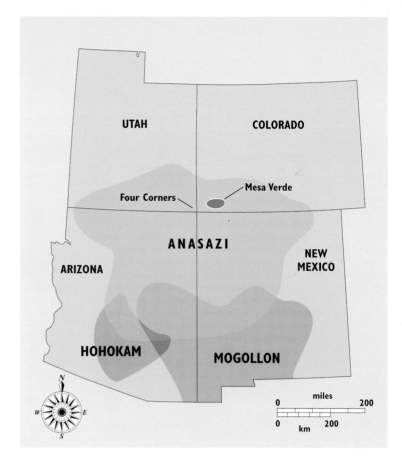

The Anasazi People of Mesa Verde

The Spanish came to the Southwest and gave Mesa Verde its name around four hundred years ago. But about a thousand years before that—before the Spanish had even heard of America—people were living on the Mesa Verde. They were the Anasazi people, and they had moved up from the dry valleys to farm on the more **fertile** mesa top. They lived on Mesa Verde for seven or eight hundred years.

People on Mesa Verde lived first in underground houses. Then they built houses above ground, joining many together to make towns. Finally, they built dwellings and even whole towns into the sides of the steep cliffs.

The Anasazi suddenly abandoned their fields on the mesa and homes in the cliffs about 1300. Nobody is quite sure why, but it probably became too dry or too dangerous to stay there. A long time later, people found the ruins of buildings and began studying the remains of Anasazi culture. That's how we know about the people who once lived on Mesa Verde.

This is the area of the United States known as the Southwest. Mesa Verde is in the Four Corners region that was home to the ancient Anasazi people.

Chapter One

The Early Anasazi

The First People in the Southwest

People first began to live in the Southwest around twelve thousand years ago. They survived by using spears to hunt bison—American buffalo—and other animals. They also ate any plant foods they could gather. The Native people of the Southwest followed the buffalo herds and lived in small groups. They lived like this for thousands of years.

These spearheads were used by Mogollon people of the Southwest for hunting game.

Finding Giant Bones

George McJunkin, once a slave in Texas, was a ranch manager near Folsom in New Mexico in 1908. That year, he found a bone sticking out of the earth at his ranch. It was the biggest bone he had ever seen. Scientists realized that it belonged to a giant bison more than ten thousand years old. When they went to the place the bone had been found, they found many more giant bones and some stone spear points made by ancient hunters. This proved that humans had lived in the area thousands of years before.

Peoples and Their Names

These first people of the Southwest gradually developed into separate groups in different regions. Around the Four Corners were the Anasazi. The Hohokam lived farther south, in the hot Arizona desert. The Mogollon were also south of the Anasazi, in New Mexico. The Hohokam and Mogollon were important to the Anasazi because they brought them ideas learned from people who lived even farther south than they did, in Mexico.

Some Native peoples have been given their names by other groups of Native people or by European settlers. When Navajo Indians came to settle in the Southwest near the Four Corners, they were the ones that gave the Anasazi their name. In the Navajo language, Anasazi means something like "ancient enemy."

The **descendants** of the Anasazi—**Pueblo** peoples such as the Hopi and Zuñi—don't like to use that name, because it isn't very friendly. They don't have a name in their own languages for their ancestors and so they call them the Ancestral Puebloans.

The ancient Native people of the Southwest, including the early Anasazi, lived in natural caves in cliffs and under rocks. This cave in the Cedar Mesa area of southwestern Utah was once an Anasazi dwelling.

Learning to Farm

Few plants grow easily without rain, and the Four Corners doesn't get much of that. Instead of relying on wild plants for food, Native people in dry parts of Mexico had started growing crops, bringing water to their fields. Very slowly, over thousands of years, the knowledge of farming worked its way north. Farming first reached southern parts of the Southwest between 2000 and 1500 B.C.

After another thousand years or so— around 500 B.C.—the Anasazi people started farming a little corn, and then squash. After their harvest, they would move to a new area. Over time, however, farming made them more settled, and corn and squash became a larger part of their diet.

A Farmer's View of His Crops

"When a person planted corn, they would be raising these corn plants up as their children. We were taught to sing to our corn, sing to our children, talk to our children, to love our children, to care for them. Corn provides us with food. It is the center of life and the essence of life."

Ramson Lomatewama, a farmer of the Zuñi people, descendants of the Anasazi

The Basketmakers

Around 1000 B.C., the Anasazi began to weave baskets from willow and other plants. They stored food in these baskets or coated their insides with **pitch** to make them watertight for carrying and storing water. People even cooked with these baskets. First they placed water and food inside. Then they dropped in stones that had been heated in the fire. The heat of the stones cooked the food.

The baskets made at this time were very beautiful, with lovely patterns and shapes. Because of the people's skill in making baskets, this period of Anasazi life—from about 100 B.C. to A.D. 700—is called the Basketmaker period.

Anasazi baskets had lovely patterns woven into them. They were very useful for storing, cooking, and carrying things.

Chapter Two

On Top of the Mesa

When the snow on Mesa Verde melted in the spring, the Anasazi used the water for farming. Water was very precious in this dry place.

Up to the Mesa
When the Anasazi began to farm, the green landscape of Mesa Verde must have looked very inviting. If trees could flourish there, why couldn't corn and squash? Sometime around A.D. 550, a number of Anasazi people climbed from the valley below to the top of the mesa and began to farm.

A Wise Choice
It was a good move. The mesa top is cooler in the summer than the valley lands below. In the winter, however, the sun reaches more of Mesa Verde than it does the shadowy valleys. So the mesa top is somewhat warmer than the lowlands in winter. This mesa also slopes south toward the warmth of the

sun, which makes the growing season on top of Mesa Verde longer. It also gets more rain and snow, which feed several springs that provide water. There is better soil than in the valleys, and the many trees provided people with wood for tools and buildings and fuel for fires.

New Tools and Resources

The Anasazi began to make mugs, pots, and other vessels by forming them out of clay and baking them in the sun. When the clay dried, the object could be used to store food or water. Since **pottery**—unlike baskets—would not burn in the campfire, the Anasazi could now cook their food properly.

The Anasazi became better farmers. They began to grow beans, a new food high in protein. People on Mesa Verde started taming wild turkeys and used their feathers to make coats and blankets.

A wild turkey living in the Arizona desert. The Anasazi people farmed turkeys for their feathers and their meat.

Turkey Troubles

"Before long [the turkeys] had added a lot more than anyone bargained for—stalking the roads and tying up traffic, raiding the gardens of staff residents, moving onto porches at the visitor center during [bad] weather and refusing to leave. They stole food, crowded inside houses when doors were left ajar, and worst of all, they [dropped dung] on everything."

Donald Pike, writing about the time when the National Park Service brought turkeys back to Mesa Verde, Anasazi: Ancient People of the Rock, *1974*

People got in and out of their pithouses by using a ladder that went through a hole in the center of the roof. The hole also let out smoke from the fire.

A New Kind of Home

A big change in the lives of the Anasazi came when they began to make their own houses instead of living in rock shelters as they had done before. Their first houses are called pithouses because they were pits dug into the ground. To make a roof, people laid tree trunks over the pit, covered them with branches and leaves, and then coated the roof with dirt.

The Beginning of the Pueblo Period

Anasazi life was slowly changing. By A.D. 700, the Anasazi were moving from the Basketmaker period into what is called the Pueblo period. In the Pueblo period, Anasazi people began to live together in larger communities. Now that they were making houses, more people could settle in the same area.

Around 750, as Anasazi people developed new **technology**, pithouses were replaced by houses built above ground. At first, their walls were made of wood covered with **adobe**. Later, people began to build their houses out of stone. The stone walls were covered with a layer of adobe and sometimes painted. Roofs were still made of wood covered with dirt.

The First Pueblos

The Anasazi became such skillful stoneworkers that soon they were making buildings joined together, two or even three and four stories high. The clustered villages looked like apartment buildings and later became known as *pueblos*, the Spanish word for "towns." That's where the Pueblo period got its name. Separate families lived in each home, but the people on Mesa Verde were living in increasingly large groups. There were sometimes hundreds of people living in one pueblo.

These are the ruins of the Far View community on Mesa Verde. Far View included nearly fifty pueblos within a half square mile (1.3 sq km). Hundreds of people lived there.

Chapter Three

Life Among the Anasazi

Today in the Southwest, Pueblo Indians such as this Hopi farmer still farm corn in the desert, much as the Anasazi did.

Daily Work

Much of the work on Mesa Verde involved growing, finding, or preparing food. Men did most of the farm work. In the spring, they cleared and planted their fields and in summer tended the growing crops. Young boys and older men watched the fields, making sure that animals did not eat the crops. In the fall, everyone helped with the harvest.

Precious Water

People made use of every drop of water. When the winter snows melted, the mesa people collected water in large pottery

jars and stored it in cool places for use later in the year. They also collected water from the natural springs on the mesa.

Anasazi men built dams on the mesa tops to hold rainwater or snowmelt that they could use to water their crops. They made **irrigation** ditches to channel water to where they needed it.

Pottery Making

Meanwhile, the women made pottery, coiling long ribbons of clay into the shape of a plate, bowl, jug, or mug. Over time, the Anasazi began to paint their pots. After drying the pot in the sun, women added a white clay coating and then painted on a design with a yucca-leaf paintbrush.

Anasazi pottery, such as this mug, ladle, and grain storage jar, were painted with juice from the beeweed plant. The juice turned black when it dried.

Flat Heads

The back of people's skulls from the Early Pueblo period are flatter than normal. Scientists believe this was caused by the way mothers used to tie their babies onto their backs. They used a hard wooden board so the babies would be secure while the women worked. Because babies' skulls are soft and easily shaped, the hard board flattened the backs of their heads. As the skull bones hardened and grew, they kept this flat shape.

In the Clan

Each family belonged to a clan, a group of families that had the same ancestors. Two members of the same clan were not allowed to marry, and children always belonged to their mother's clan. Each clan had its own special animal, such as a badger or a turtle. Clans played an important role in Anasazi **spiritual** life.

When the Anasazi began building above-ground houses, they continued to make underground buildings, too. These were *kivas*, which are special chambers for religious ceremonies. It is likely that each clan had its own kiva and that only men were allowed inside.

The great kiva at Pueblo Bonito in Chaco Canyon, shown here, would have been a gathering place for people from many clans. You can see the round hole of the sipapu in the foreground. Originally, the kiva would have had a roof.

The Kiva

People entered kivas through the roof as they had done when they lived in pithouses. There was a fireplace in the center and there were stone benches around the walls. In the floor of the kiva was a hole now known as a *sipapu*. Historians think the sipapu has to do with Native American stories of creation. The stories say that the first humans were born inside the Earth and crawled out of a hole in the ground.

These **petroglyphs** found in Navajo Canyon on Mesa Verde show people, animals, and spiral patterns that may represent the movement of the Sun. They may have had spiritual meaning or simply be records of hunting triumphs, good harvests, or conflicts.

A Southwestern Creation Story

"In the beginning two female human beings were born. There was land already, but no one knows how long it existed. The two girls were born underground at a place called Cipapu. There was no light. . . . [The spirit] said, 'You have the seeds of four types of trees. Plant them; you will use the trees to climb up.' . . . A certain pine grew faster than the others, and after a very long while it pushed a hole through the earth and let in a little light.

"'It is time for you to go out,' [the spirit] said. 'When you come to the top, wait for the sun to rise. . . . Pray to the sun . . . with pollen and sacred cornmeal, which you will find in your baskets. Thank it for bringing you to the light. Ask for long life and happiness, and for success in the purpose for which you were created.'"

Creation story of the Ácoma people of New Mexico,
American Indian Myths and Legends

Chapter Four

Moving to the Cliffs

Cliff Palace is the largest Anasazi cliff dwelling site found on Mesa Verde. It had more than two hundred rooms and twenty-three kivas. The cave holding Cliff Palace is more than 320 feet (98 m) long, nearly 90 feet (27 m) deep, and almost 60 feet (18 m) high.

The Cliff Towns

In the 1100s, the Mesa Verde people were moving into larger communities. They were becoming even more skillful at making stonework and pottery.

In the 1200s, however, the people of Mesa Verde suddenly made yet another change. Many of them left the mesa top and began to build homes in the cliffs that formed the sides of Mesa Verde. The cliffs have many caves large enough to hold buildings and whole villages.

Up and Down the Cliffs

Living on the cliffs must have been very difficult. Historians don't think there were any paths leading to the mesa tops or

Why Did They Move?

Why did the Mesa Verde people move into cliff dwellings? No one knows. Some historians say it was because of troubles in the Anasazi region in these years. Living in the sides of the cliffs may have given the Anasazi protection from enemies.

Others think that the move to the cliffs was a sign of overcrowding or lack of food on the mesa top. By moving homes off the mesa tops, the Anasazi left more land there to be farmed. Also, the overhanging cliffs shielded people and their houses from wind, rain, and snow.

the canyon bottoms. The only way to get up and down was by climbing the sheer rock—the fingerholds and toeholds that the Anasazi cut into the cliff face are still there. People had to climb in this way even while hauling food and supplies into their towns. Children and older people tended to stay close to home because the climb out of the cliffside home was so risky.

At Long House, these buildings were fitted right into the back of the cave to use all the available space. Surrounding these existing walls would have been other walls and other rooms. The whole space was very crowded.

The Buildings

Most of these cliff settlements were small, holding homes for only a few families, but some were huge. Long House had about 150 rooms and 21 kivas. Spruce Tree House had nearly 120 rooms and 8 kivas. The dwellings were built in the same way as they had been on top of the mesa, but now people had to carry building materials up and down the cliffs.

Living on the Cliffs

Life was probably quite crowded in the cliff dwellings. Cooking was not done inside the homes but outside, on rooftops. The homes had no windows and only one small doorway, so cooking inside would have filled the room with smoke. Some historians think that cliff dwellers did not build fires inside their homes for the same reason, and so it was very cold and damp in winter.

Rooms in the back of the town were used to store food for the winter as well as seed to plant for the following year's

Garbage was a problem in the cliff dwellings. One site to dump trash was any space between the backs of the buildings and the inner wall of the cave. Another dump was the area in front of the village. **Archaeologists** digging in loose piles of **debris** in front of cliff buildings have found sandals, broken pottery, tools made of bone or stone, and corn cobs. These are leftovers of Anasazi life.

Anasazi debris found at Eagle Nest cliff dwelling in Lion Canyon, Colorado.

crops. The tamed turkeys came to cliff villages, too. They were allowed to walk through the town during the day, but at night they were enclosed at the back.

Health in the Cliff Dwellings

Conditions in the towns, as in the rest of the world at the time, were not very **hygienic**. Some rooms toward the back of the towns were apparently used as toilets. These conditions might have led to increased sickness. Diseases would spread easily with lack of hygiene in a closed space.

Anasazi bodies have been found in garbage piles at cliff sites. The bodies show that many Anasazi people suffered from arthritis and had bad backs. Dental problems were common, too. The cornmeal people ate was rough and gritty —it wore away at their teeth, causing cavities and infections. Historians believe that most Anasazi who survived through early childhood then died in their fifties. They would die from sickness, wounds, or infections for which they had no cure.

Chapter Five

Mysteries and Discoveries

Anasazi people left things behind on Mesa Verde and elsewhere in the Four Corners region. These Anasazi earrings were found hundreds of years after they were made.

A Time of Famine

"At last the corn was all gone. The people were pitiably poor. They were so weak that they could not hunt through the snow, therefore a great famine spread through the village. At last the people were compelled to gather old bones and grind them for meal."

Zuñi people's legend about a period of drought among their ancestors, quoted in Brian Fagan, Time Detectives, *1995*

Leaving the Mesa

In the late 1200s or early 1300s, the Anasazi suddenly disappeared. They left Mesa Verde and most other parts of the Four Corners region.

The Anasazi left not just their homes, but many of their possessions. People exploring the cliff towns in the late 1800s found many pieces of pottery, yucca sandals, jewelry, and other things.

No one knows exactly why people left Mesa Verde. But historians have found out that from 1276, the area began to suffer from a serious **drought**. Year after

year, there was little snow and rain. It would have been almost impossible to continue to survive.

Where Did They Go?

People used to think the Anasazi had all died off. But today, archaeologists and historians believe that the people of Mesa Verde—along with other Anasazi people—simply moved south and settled on other lands. Many of them settled in the valley of the Rio Grande in present-day New Mexico. Others settled in western New Mexico or eastern Arizona.

A Boom in the South

"About AD 1300 three families moved into an area above a spring and founded Arroyo Hondo [a site near what is now Santa Fe, New Mexico]. Within thirty years the population had soared to fifteen hundred. The same happened all along this stretch of the [Rio Grande]."

Dr. Douglas W. Schwartz, archaeologist, who studies the resettlement of the Anasazi

Unearthing an Anasazi pot, as this archaeologist is doing in Arizona, is a rare and exciting event today. Most sites have already had their treasures removed.

Deserted

Back on Mesa Verde, as the years passed, weather damaged the abandoned homes. The roofs of kivas collapsed, and winds knocked down stones that had once formed the walls of houses. Trees and shrubs once more grew across the mesa top, covering those areas that had been farmland.

Finding Clues

The Anasazi did not write their history in books. How, then, do we know so much about them? Fragments of stone tools, pottery, and turkey-feather robes have been found in ancient sites. They give us clues about Anasazi life. Bones at camp sites show what animals the Anasazi hunted. The remains of corn cobs show that they ate corn and that they were farmers.

Few **artifacts** of the Anasazi life remain at Mesa Verde today. Archaeologists may find broken bits of pottery. When they are very lucky, they find an entire bowl or basket.

Date Detectives

A tree's growth every year is shown by the pattern of rings in its trunk. Scientists use tree rings to tell them the age of ancient buildings and artifacts. They can take a sample of wood from an Anasazi site and, by counting its rings, figure out how old each Anasazi site is.

Tree rings also reveal how much rain fell in any year in the past. When a lot of rain fell, the tree rings from that year are wide. In years of little rain, the rings are very narrow and close together. Tree rings told scientists about the many years of drought in the late 1200s.

Tree ring samples from a giant sequoia help this scientist understand the tree's history.

Conclusion

At an Indian ceremony in Taos Pueblo, New Mexico, the dancers are wearing traditional feathered costumes. Pueblo people are famous for their dances.

The Pueblo People

"Pueblo Indians" is the name sometimes used for people of the Southwest today. The Pueblo peoples include the Hopi, the Zuñi, the Laguna, and the Ácoma. Most historians agree that some of the Pueblo Indians of Arizona and New Mexico are the descendants of the Anasazi who moved south in the late 1200s and early 1300s. These Pueblo peoples live in apartment-like pueblos, as the Anasazi had. They farm using some of the same methods as the Anasazi. Their kivas are similar to the kivas of Mesa Verde and other Anasazi sites.

The modern Pueblo people feel a deep connection to the ancient Anasazi. As one Zuñi man says, "The Anasazi are well and happy in the Rio Grande valley."

Changing and Staying the Same

Even today, Pueblo people keep ancient spiritual beliefs alive. Like other Americans, they have accepted modern things, but the Pueblo people have managed to keep their traditional culture, too.

Some pueblos have become well known for their arts and crafts. The Hopis, for instance, make beautiful sculptures of carved, painted wood that represent ceremonial spiritual figures. Artists from a number of pueblos are known for their hand-crafted pottery. Even today—as in the times of the ancient Anasazi—these artists use yucca leaves to paint patterns on their pots.

A National Treasure

In 1906, a big part of Mesa Verde was made into a national park. Thousands of visitors come to the park each year, where they can see sites such as the Far View pueblos. On the cliffs, visitors to the ruins at Cliff Palace, Long House, and Spruce Tree House can imagine what life was like hundreds of years ago.

Our Land

"This has always been our land. We know these matters not merely because our grandparents told us vague stories when we were children, but because our parents and grandparents, and their parents and grandparents before them, made sure to tell us so exactly and so often that we could not forget."

Elders of the Zia, Jemez, and Santa Ana groups in the Southwest, in a petition to the federal government to claim land, 1950

The Anasazi settlement of Balcony House is just as hard to reach as it was two thousand years ago. Visitors use ladders installed by Mesa Verde National Park to reach the site.

Time Line

500 B.C.	Anasazi begin to farm.
100 B.C.	Beginning of Basketmaker period: farming corn and squash plus hunting and gathering.
A.D. 400	Beginning of Late Basketmaker period: farming beans, making pottery, making pithouses.
550	Anasazi begin settlements on Mesa Verde.
700	Beginning of Pueblo period: building above-ground houses.
900	Kivas begin to appear on Mesa Verde.
1200	Anasazi on Mesa Verde begin building homes on cliffside sites.
1276	First of many years of severe drought on Mesa Verde.
1300	Mesa Verde is abandoned.
1540s	Spanish first reach the Southwest.
1906	Most of Mesa Verde is named a national park.

Things to Think About and Do

Living in the Cliffs

Imagine you are an Anasazi child living in a cliff dwelling on Mesa Verde. Write a few paragraphs describing an ordinary day: what you do, what you eat, what your home is like, the weather, and the dangers and challenges of where you live.

The Anasazi and the Pueblo Peoples

Find out more about the Pueblo Indian peoples such as the Hopi, Zuñi, and Ácoma, or the people that live along the Rio Grande. Compare aspects of their lives with what you have learned about the Anasazi. You could look at clothes, food, farming methods, spiritual life, and housing. What is the same and what is different?

The Year 4000

Imagine you are an archaeologist in the year 4000. You have discovered the ancient ruins of a settlement from the year 2000. Describe some of the artifacts you find there, what you think they are, and what they tell you about the culture of the people who lived two thousand years before you.

Glossary

adobe: building material made of mud and dried in the sun.

archaeologist: person who studies remains of earlier human cultures.

artifact: something that was made by humans and still exists from an earlier time.

debris: remains and leftovers. Often used to mean crumbled rock from broken buildings as well as other remains.

descendant: person who comes in a later generation in a family.

drought: period with much less rainfall than normal, causing shortages of water.

fertile: good for growing plants.

hygienic: very clean and without germs.

irrigation: a method of bringing water to fields and gardens.

mortar: paste made of clay and water used by the Anasazi to hold stone in place.

petroglyph: manmade carving, usually consisting of images, in rock surface.

pitch: thick liquid made from the sap of some trees. When spread over a surface and left to dry, pitch makes the surface waterproof.

pottery: object such as a bowl, drinking vessel, or container made of wet clay. The object is dried so it hardens and keeps its shape.

pueblo: Spanish word for "town." In the Southwest it refers to the apartment-like, clustered towns of the Native people. "Pueblo Indians" is the collective name given to various groups of Native people living in the Southwest.

spiritual: having to do with sacred or religious things.

technology: knowledge and ability that improve ways of doing practical things.

yucca: plant found in the Southwest that has a long, thick stem with stiff leaves around the base and flowers at the top.

Further Information

Books

Bartok, Mira and Christine Ronan. *Pueblo Indians of the Southwest* (Ancient and Living Cultures: Stencils). Goodyear, 2000.

Goodman, Susan E. *Stones, Bones, and Petroglyphs: Digging into Southwest Archaeology.* Atheneum, 1998.

McDermott, Gerald. *Arrow to the Sun: A Pueblo Indian Tale.* Viking, 1974.

Sita, Lisa. *Indians of the Southwest: Traditions, History, Legends, and Life.* Gareth Stevens, 2001.

Young, Robert. *A Personal Tour of Mesa Verde.* (How It Was Series). Lerner, 1999.

Web Sites

www.cliffdwellingsmuseum.com/anasazi Good information about the Anasazi people from web site of the Manitou Cliff Dwellings.

www.co.blm.gov/ahc/artifact.htm Anasazi Heritage Center displays ancient artifacts from Mesa Verde and other Anasazi sites.

www.nps.gov/meve/ Mesa Verde National Park offers practical information about the park and the Anasazi sites to be found there.

Useful Addresses

Mesa Verde National Park
P.O. Box 8
Mesa Verde, CO 81330
Telephone: (970) 529-4465

Anasazi Heritage Center
27501 Highway 184
Dolores, CO 81323
Telephone: (970) 882-4811

Index